MRS PERKINS AND OEDIPUS

Elizabeth Bartlett was born in 1924 in Deal, in the mining region of Kent. She left school at 15 shortly before the start of the Second World War, to start work in a factory making hypodermic needles. Married during the War, she helped support her family with various jobs, working for 16 years as a medical secretary, and later in the home help service and as a tutor. (w\ E\A)

Despite early success at the age of 19, in Tambimuttu's *Poetry London*, she did not publish again until her mid-50s. Her first retrospective volume, *A Lifetime of Dying: Poems 1942-1979* (Peterloo Poets, 1979), covered mainly work written in the latter two decades. She went on to publish four collections in the 1980s and early 90s: *Strange Territory* (Peterloo Poets, 1983), *The Czar Is Dead* (Rivelin Grapheme, 1986), *Instead of a Mass* (Headland, 1991) and *Look, No Face* (Redbeck Press, 1991). In 1995 Bloodaxe published *Two Women Dancing: New & Selected Poems*, edited by Carol Rumens, which was a Poetry Book Society Recommendation, followed by *Appetites of Love* in 2001, and now *Mrs Perkins and Oedipus*, published on her 80th birthday, 28 April 2004.

Frances with love from

ELIZABETH BARTLETT

Elizabeth
2004

Mrs Perkins
AND
Oedipus

BLOODAXE BOOKS

Copyright © Elizabeth Bartlett 2004

ISBN: 1 85224 668 5

First published 2004 by
Bloodaxe Books Ltd,
Highgreen,
Tarset,
Northumberland NE48 1RP.

www.bloodaxebooks.com
For further information about Bloodaxe titles
please visit our website or write to
the above address for a catalogue.

Bloodaxe Books Ltd acknowledges
the financial assistance of
Arts Council England, North East.

Cover printing by J. Thomson Colour Printers Ltd, Glasgow.

Printed in Great Britain by
Cromwell Press Ltd, Trowbridge, Wiltshire.

For Pam and Veronica,
for teaching me how
to be a widow

ACKNOWLEDGEMENTS

Acknowledgements are due to the editors of the following publications where some of these poems first appeared: *Ambit, Envoi, The Interpreter's House, The North, Outposts, Poetry London, Poetry Review, The Rialto, Thumbscrew, Van Gogh's Ear* (France) and *The Welsh Review*.

CONTENTS

Staring into the Abyss

When they rang to say you were dead
I thought only of freedom and no chilly
Heaven with obligatory harps and angels,
or even your first wife to greet you there
after leaving you for her lover.

I only thought of Goya's black paintings
you inhabited for far too long,
or your arrival in Dante's circles in Hell,
or King Lear's wild raving as you wandered
round the house, searching for what?

We gathered at the crematorium in midwinter.
Our son dressed in his black M&S suit,
my stepchildren and their children,
the usual twentieth-century pattern of double lives,
there to see him off at the last.

The green cardboard coffin, the one bouquet
of flowers, the small posy of hazel catkins
and mahonia flowers, stood as if on a stage
and we were the audience, your exit
as dignified as you used to be,

before Alzheimers claimed you, before
the house of horrors, labelled E.M.I.
cared for by strangers at the last
and not knowing who I was
or why I visited you and why I cried.

I read your novels and your journals
which are all I have of you,
and wear your socks and jerseys
to keep me warm, give back the zimmer,
the commode, the incontinence pads,
and weep, for what you were; and I have lost.

Trouble in the Balkans

It was always there,
his father's despair
as he fondled the gun,
his mother's as she made
the noose she hung
in the bedroom,
which became a dying room.

The same thoughts they had
must have come unsought
to the thousands, traversing
the bitter landscape of Kosovo,
watched on our TV's daily.
Babyface, orphan Sloba,
dysfunctional family.

To him it feels familiar;
the shot priest his father,
the teacher of young children
swinging from the light fitting.
His lights go out one by one.
This is a scenario he knows
deep inside himself, his country.

NOTE: Milosovic's parents both committed suicide.

Dear Boy

Dear boy, I said, what you need
is a PLAN; sort out your priorities
if you can. I was Head of Department,
knew my way around; if you heed
what I say, who knows where you might
end up, a man like me perhaps.

There was nothing I didn't know about
freight and figures, even the commissionaire
wept when I left. I called him Bob
to show I wasn't a man to forget
that an ordinary man is just as rare
as me (to his wife, perhaps, or kids.)
Look – er – Fred, I used to say, it's all
in the mind. Well, he was pathetic
really and in the executive bar we'd fall
about laughing at the way he stood there,
just opening and shutting the door
for us, the backbone of the company.

Dear boy, I said to the man I hired
to re-sand the parquet in the lounge,
I was Smith of the P.Q.R., you need
to watch what you say or you're fired.
He worked for himself it seemed.
I felt a bit odd that morning, newly retired,
but I know my stuff. Next day, early,
I took him on one side and said
I hadn't been serious about my warning,
that he could be head of a building firm
if he knew the right way to talk
and dress and learned how to play golf.
Turned out he was a Cambridge man,
liked using his hands he said, and May
balls and High Table were not for him.
He hadn't heard of the P.Q.R,
but he made a good job of the floor,
I'll say that for him, and when he left
I opened the door. Goodbye Laurence:
Larry, he said. Watching him go
I felt ill at ease and almost bereft.

Secondaries

You are like a lover who remembers
to call me back after the affair is over.
You own me, and you know my body well,
each little anatomical detail, and not only
the skin but the channels and runnels,
the lymph glands and the stalks of the polyps.

I sit on the edge of the bed, raging,
biting my lip, bawling like a child.
You are so like my father, wanting
my hair to fall out to curb my vanity,
sickness to curb my greed, uncertainty
to jolt me out of habit and routine,
something to demonstrate the subtle art
of battle, trench warfare, a waiting game.

I wear my striped pants like any inmate
of a death camp and read Updike overtly
in the waiting-room. Sod you, I think,
I never thought you'd come back for me.
You are my enemy and I will not let you
own me; my father and I will not let you
call me daughter. If you are any kind
of lover, take your chilly palms off me
and watch me flirting with the doctor.

We are old hands and used to this,
(his bypass surgery, my bloody little
seeding heads). They are eager now
for new borders, stealthy invaders.
Get out the weed killer, I say. He laughs.
Really, we could die laughing.

Before Meeting

Again, again, the tinny convent bell implores,
the idle leaf fidgets in the cold courtyard,
a nun empties the sodden tea-leaves
under the purple-plumed lilac;
and outside, children spin dice on the pavement
with the salesman from Chicago.

Domine non sum dignus,
and the maiden candles
flutter and dribble their flesh
on scarlet and threaded gold
and the tasselled cloth;
the hectic-cheeked madonna
stiffly cradles our plaster child;
and the Irish navvy
spits his way
through the delicate litanies.

But I have a chanting and prayer,
I offer up my invocations
under his great glad archway,
I shall become my own white lovely dice
under the hard hands
of the crouching figure
from Chicago.

Recorder Consort

This church has the long-forgotten smell
of dust and damp and mice; the bell
hangs silent in the tower, the harsh
curtain swings in the doorway.
On alien, echoing feet
we move through gaudy sun-lit patterns
of heraldic blue and red, and find a seat
where even the ungodly may sit
to listen.

Where is the unuttered word for the plaint
of recorders playing in consort, curving round
the naked pillars in bright ribbons of sound
which twist and plait and untie,
and die, and rise, and fall, and interweave
in elaborate contexture?
The music grows like a quickthorn and trembles
like a tracery of grasses in a pewter jug
against the many years lost walls
of wattle and daub.

Through the beat of the hollow fluting I go,
past the tavern doors and over the uneven floors;
I dance in the brittle court, eaten fast
away by intrigue, and in flea-ridden
domestic simplicity. A recorder lies
among the rushes, and the smell of mice
and damp scatters the centuries
as we sit surrounded and ravished
by this gentle tumult.

Smarty

It is a detached house, sporting
a vulgar clematis by the door,
with a drive full of cars, screened
off from the road. She sports her class
with her name and her impeccable
antecedents, the independent school
she went to and the good manners
she deploys with pleading words
and confident gestures.

I have been here before and seen
only the servants' quarters, but now
I come as a member of the middle classes,
except that I erupt in a brutal language
which offends and sends her scattering
retaliatory words like seeds,
'You are *horrid*,' she says, '*not nice.*'

I thumb my nose and depart, laughing
to myself and humming 'The Red Flag'
under my breath, a smart-arsed kid,
slung out on my ear and glad.

Grand Mal

The aura may be an intense feeling of despair
and sadness lasting for some hours, or on the air
the smell of carnations, before the eleven seconds
count down, and the shaking jerking fit,
the fall into nothingness. The spittle and urine
trickle away as the spasms get less, the teeth
release their hold from the tongue at last,
which feels bruised and swollen in the mouth.

Returning, he sits up and the faces gaze down.
He is ashamed to be so wet and dishevelled
and sleepy. There is an air of concern
and a turning away too. He disappears
and yet is all too evidently there to see,
frantic as an injured insect on the floor,
upsetting the onlookers. He is upset himself
and has no friends, for they are afraid.

Standing by the playground walls, the children
say 'I nearly had a fit', then clap their hands
to their mouths. In his six years
he cannot understand why they do not smell
those violent carnations, or how they
have time to undo their zips, or keep
their tongues so sleek and fresh and pink,
and get asked to parties and to tea.

The Way He Had

(in memoriam James Bartlett, 1909-86)

When you rang to say
that James was dead
I thought of climbing
into his head and shaking him
awake, pulling back
the fag-scorched blankets
from the iron bed.
Hero and lover, his blazer
thrown upon a chair,
his tennis racquets
in the shed,
ash in his hair.
I thought I'd marry
someone like Jim,
but there was nobody
quite like him.

When you rang to say
the time would be
eleven and the day
was fixed
I thought of the way
he used to play
the pub piano
in our front parlour.
Tickling the ivories
was a thirties phrase.
He was a thirties man,
when I was a lonely kid
and he was a college boy.
I remember Jim,
and the way he had
with him.

Castle Park, Nottingham

It is, after all, what your grandmother
would call a nice class of neighbourhood.
Riding on the coat tails of Nottingham castle,
she has some bother with burglars nicking
the family silver, sidling quietly away
into pools of darkness between the gas lamps.
She fears they might be what she calls
coloured, and patently up to no good;
they certainly left her a darker shade
of pale, cutting the windows so neatly
and choosing only the best forks and spoons.
She wonders who could be using them now,
and imagines great lumps of meat spiked
in neighbourhoods which are not as nice
as Castle Park, touching the lips
of people she's afraid to give a name,
in case they come to visit her again.

Burying Browne

Havana cats. This chestnut-brown short-hair with the fine oriental body is about as Cuban as a London bobby. It was developed in England by breeding from the offspring of Siamese and short-haired British.
FRANK MANOLSON

The fourth cat grave in a small garden,
he dug it on his knees to save his back.
Division of labour was part of their lives,
so she had taken the thin bag of bones
and fur to the vet, rescued him from that
hideous back room where stiffening bodies lay
in heaps ready for the skin-trade's van
to call next day.

They had mocked him in his decade of life,
'A brown blancmange, an owl in bear's clothes',
and regretted their laughter and the words
he never understood. Warmth he had, and this
he understood. Food he had, and this also
he waited for at the altar of the pantry door.
All he left behind was the smell of urine
and a puzzled stare.

We saw him off decent, she wanted to say,
as he piled on the earth, the heavy yellow clay.
Second-best, the timid wary one, he wore
the best soft brown coat, and was surprisingly
vocal, but died with a terrible patient silence,
turning his head from side to side, groaning
under his breath, waiting for Easter to pass
for the merciful needle.

Not so very different, they both thought soberly
from the lives of ordinary people, holding down
badly paid jobs, glad of shelter and bread.
You might say he had his private quiet bed,
his willing nurse, lay where he had hesitantly
wandered, but knew his place, a cushion
for the Siamese prince to recline upon,
the butt of sardonic jokes.

A Death in Summer

Out of the quiet combings of stained clouds,
and children's voices trapped in the interstices
of the hedge, and weeds withering on the path
comes a jungle message of drum-beating feet
and a sudden exit in the misty powerful heat
into nothing sitting up in bed staring
at no Present from Brighton, wearing
incongruous striped pyjamas, an old man
dead in the evening, pillows propping a heedless back,
the wall-eyed telly flickering on in the corner
like a forgotten idiot chained to a table out of the way.

After the brief silence of incredulity
come the gargling sobs and the doctor's visit,
swinging his useless stethoscope he walks away,
soap and a mackintosh sheet are borrowed now,
and, like the child they belong to, he is tidied
and washed and made to lie down for the flames
to receive him and the scent of flowers to fill
his unassailable nostrils. In the dark corner
someone takes the idiot by the hand, turning the knob
they lead him away, and the wall-eye closes
on a sudden death in summer.

Royal Ottoman

We are just back from *Royal Ottoman*,
after four thousand years of history
and more than a touch of winter sun.

We flew to Vienna, Istanbul, Luxor, Cairo, Rome
for the price of a modest roll-ragged decor,
show off our tan when we arrive home.

Air cruising, we hardly saw the sleazy
back streets and what we lost in Istanbul
we found again in Luxor. It was easy

to imagine ourselves back in the years
before 1919 (the year our parents married),
as we ate our kebabs with a barbarous ease.

Somewhere in our father's dusty rooms
there was an ottoman we opened at last,
finding it as empty as a ransacked tomb.

Voyage for the Incurious

I set my little Mary statue
on the fire-shelf in a sea-village,
Brighton-bought plaster maiden
in a land of chapels.

On one side, the ripe beauty
of the Italian jar,
blue and yellow,
broad, like the hips of a woman
with child walking alone
along the leafy streets
of green vineyards
in a land of lachrymae Christi
and dirty madonnas.
Filled with grass is it,
and shouting with yellow stalks
of barley gathered in August
from Dyffrynsaith fields,
where the stooks sing separation
on the gentle mountain.

My gilded girl, coldly painted,
slim as a city tart,
stands delitescent, untainted,
against grey walls;
and the glass ball
that greenly rolled
in the frothy curve
of Cardigan Bay
shines green, shines bright
on her right hand,
cool smooth, cool round,
thrown up by the sea.

In the sea-whisper shell
of the afternoon
war fades,
but the marram binds
the comber-beaten shore

with frenzied fingers,
sings separation, separation.
Mute, the room-reflecting ball,
the colour-rutted jar,
the childless Mary,
wait with me
for the next voyage.

Nothing Much Happened to Emily

I don't go anywhere, so how do I know anything?
This is a false statement. I cycle to work, I ring.

my bell, I grieve, uneasy on my split saddle, over
corpses of hedgehogs, small birds, squirrels.

A car comes up behind me and knocks me down.
I am unhurt, but the driver examines me with a look

which says only too plainly that a woman should ride
in a straight line and not turn aside to avoid

small animals. I go to classes too, in the dark,
walking with my head full of words and Emily.

Coming home, a man paces behind me. He stops
when I stop, he moves when I move. I turn

into a shadowed drive, pretending it is mine,
and wait until he tires of predatory games.

Nothing much happens; it just nearly happens,
and then, like a shaken kaleidoscope resolves

itself into different patterns. Nothing much
happened to Emily. Nothing really happens to me.

It's just Amherst revisited.

Scholarship Girl

Stunned at school, to hear a German carol sung to her father's tune,
it took a long time to unravel the Red Flag from Tannenbaum.

Similarly, her Co-op uniform betrayed her, for it was not the outfitter
the school preferred, her darned black stockings looked all wrong.

In her excitement at the marvellous things she encountered there,
she dropped her h's, shot up her hand and called her mistress 'miss'.

Dragged up in front of the class she swiftly learned the maiden lady's
name and practised her aspirates assiduously in front of the mirror.

It all paid off in the end. She climbed to the top of the class rapidly,
and the dentist's and bank manager's daughters wondered what had
        hit them.

Pale and undernourished though she looked, her mother fed her well,
but feared TB. So many of the family had died of it in the past.

She even cashed in on this, coughing discreetly behind the pages
of Rupert Brooke, was excused games, wore her hat brim turned up.

That this was against the rules pleased her, so she also tore off
the school's woven badge and said she'd lost it on the morning train.

Later, writing the kind of poetry few editors would stick their necks
out for, she stalked about like a bean-pole, thumbing her nose.

Her middle-class voice, manipulated carefully, sometimes evaded her,
and people's shins got kicked when they were least expecting it.

Student as Cat Rumpler

Jean-Pierre Rumple, you call the bouncer,
and Jelly Roll Morton the chocolate mousse
who forms himself into subservient
and unappealing shapes around your feet.
Rumpling is a form of stomach rubbing,
Bartokian, if done to music, brief
if done on the way to the long essay,
and the application form for a research grant.
Jean-Pierre offers himself for rumpling,
fawn belly stretched in anticipation;
Jelly Roll is half afraid, sometimes
lies down as if to be a bouncer,
changes his mind, and licks his paws.
Family jokes, ephemera, gone so soon,
until student as cat rumpler
is owned by another cat and passes
the message on,
Quia ego nominor leo.

Night Nurse

There's the church, built in red brick,
(the Unitarian is decked in pink and white
these days), the Adult Education Centre
with its portico and the tarted-up stable block.
Middlemarch on Tuesdays, Psychology today.
Unlike the American Professor, the M.Sc. is thin;
'delightfully emaciated' I write in my journal,
'like an approachable but pint-sized Freud'.
Marian was a bit of an old boiler herself,
and no oil painting. How do they teach this
in E.F.L.? Bernard can't get his tongue
round that one and X sees freeze-frames
of *Le Chat dans le sac* in bed at night.
'Never wanted to' she diligently hums. Again.
Pragmatic morning alters all those surreal fantasies
into something quite acceptable, like love,
regret, the lonely portioning out of hours,
cigarettes like commas, drinks like semi-colons,
the sleeping tablet a round white full-stop.
Goodbye Jim Augustin. You were only a bit part,
translated from the Tagalog under stress.
Should you put farts into your poems, I wonder?
The letters from Manila Metro keep arriving;
old songs, old films seen again on the TV
soothe me like a night nurse after evening classes.

Runcimans, Cheltenham

It is so discreet, at first it is
hard to discern. It is as if the drink
is hidden like drugs in gold bars.
It doesn't bother to open on time,
and no space invaders whine in corners.
Wine is consumed in Georgian glasses
and no pub sign swings in the wind.
Only respectable people go to Runcimans.
'It makes one want to swear or scream,'
he says. She drops her matches on the floor.
'Bloody hell,' she says, but quietly,
as someone gently pushes the wooden door.
It wouldn't be right to have a row
in Runcimans for walls have ears,
or so they say. It doesn't do to part
in a place like Runcimans.

A Mad Dublin Man

I didn't think I'd meet him there,
swearing like a trooper, flicking his ash
over the pristine carpet, filling the room
with his loud voice, flexing his muscles
behind the drawn lace curtains,
as if he had every right to be there.
Itinerant Irish navvy, he might be
a terrorist or just one of the mad
Dublin men drinking in bars,
wearing their working clothes,
predatory, coarse and dirty,
secretly tending a cache of Semtex
somewhere in some remote suburb.

I am afraid of him, of what he will
do, scared as I am of my own shadow
these days. I block my ears against
the noise of his persuasive voice,
hollering in my ears; the smell of him
is all pervading. I shall shower him
off me, when I get home, place food
on my pine table, feed the cats,
say my prayers. *Hail Mary Mother of God.*
I finger my rosary like a convent girl,
although I left so long ago,
and cross myself over and over
to keep away the dark.

On Dover Beach

(after Matthew Arnold)

We are swanning up and down
the promenade, beauty and the beast.
She is pretty and clever and I am
ugly but also clever, my frown
of concentration gets me to the top
of the class, her velvety eyes
and widow's peak get her boyfriends.

Suddenly, among the holiday crowds,
the blackshirts come for the summer,
strutting round our seaside town,
alien and exciting, handing out
pamphlets and sexy as hell,
but we are only schoolgirls
in scuffed sandals and cotton frocks.
We don't stand a chance,
but neither do they, eventually.

The men we married squashed them
under their heels like cockroaches,
wearing black army boots and khaki shirts.
Dead sexy.

Interview

(for and after Simon Armitage)

You wanted to run up and down
the road in this unremarkable town
and knock on the neighbour's doors
to tell them Simon Armitage peed
in your loo today, walked on your floors.
He was sat on your sofa-bed-today,
(not much good as a sofa, less
as a bed). Simon who? they'd say.
He is the man from the BBC,
judging a half century of fruit
to be ready for picking,
like the Del Monte man.
He has brown eyes and brown boots
and just the right kind of
nineties hair.

Remembering his bad back, I ask
after it. Not too bad, he says.
Simon, born 1963, had a pee,
asked questions and went away,
back up North, all in one day.

Our twelve year old spotted tabby
uses the bath like a commode.
You hope he didn't think
you condone this. You hope
her kittens don't copy her.
You hope he gets home safely.
You hope he doesn't read this.

The Poet's House

This is the house, with doors
a faded shade of blue.
She lived here for a long time;
more than thirty years,
with rush-mats on all the floors
and a bottle of vodka under the bed;
books and papers everywhere,
an untidy frowsty lair.

What went on in her head
was somehow like the dusty rooms
she wandered through,
listlessly looking for the one clue
which would make the scribbled poems
jerk into life and show
themselves to her as she waited.
They are still here, undated,
like bird's claw prints in the snow,
waiting for the thaw to come
and the western winds to blow.

Now she is gone, the grabbing hands
Pluck her as she fades from memory
and drum her into reluctant life again.
Coating her with printer's ink
and noting her last nervous blink,
they scuttle off with browning pages,
making money out of pain.

A Summer Settlement

There was rain in the night,
washing away the stillborn poems
left at the valley-bottom yesterday,
children who never jerked into life,
or howled at the toppling chimneys.

Some of the babies are doing well,
slapped smartly into shape on the keys
of a typewriter. They were conceived
a long time ago in another country
which holds a different passport.

Two people are taking a post-natal
walk to Heptonstall, the blackened stone
chapelry which never found a name
until Hebden stall and holds echoes
of virgin births and cuckolding.

Half the night, listening to the rain,
there were a lot of easy labours,
and disposing of placentas, but some
births took their toll, eclampsia
flashing off in fits and starts.

This summer settlement is where
they all migrated to, one parent families
who will give away their children
to the first person who offers a home,
already intent on the next gestation.

The abortionist has a tight smile
as he carefully covers the small
evidences of a line or two juxtaposed
and finally crossed out. He aims
to keep the population down if he can.

The mill owner looks down as they depart –
the literary girls in crumpled cotton skirts,
the men in pre-shrunk jeans. The midwives
pack their bags; words stiffen like cloth,
the hawk's wings darkening the sky.

Male Lifers

Cutting across bleak country,
through the narrow lanes,
guilty of a few mild crimes,
like nicking from Woolworths
or shooting off my mouth too often,
I am afraid of the boisterous screws
laughing in the corridor outside:
on the wrong side yet again.

Coming in from the needles of rain,
it is all deceptively peaceful;
men with blanched faces and long hair,
carefully rolling thin cigarettes,
and the rapt attentive gaze
as my eyes meet theirs.
I am the first to look away
from their look of concealed pain.

Firing from the hip, I begin
to read, carelessly murdering
the English language and forgetting
where I am and who they are,
as the adrenalin begins to flow
like life-blood through my veins,
armed with my weaponry of words
and my victim's stains.

Leaving, I say I'll come again,
and shiver in the cold night air.
The mist is rising from the valley
as the floodlights slice the sky,
and I hear a soft and melancholy moaning
all round the perimeter fence.
I do not believe it is the wind's
objective and perpetual refrain.

Clapper Bridge

The shallow pool slackens
as it crosses the road way,
and then flows smoothly
among the rocks and stones
under hanging branches
of grey sallow.

The clapper footbridge echoes
with your steps, your hand
on the iron handrail, your boots
laced correctly.
No one knows quite who built it,
with no opening ceremony.

Up the combe a buzzard soars
and wheels, just once,
gentians like blue thimbles,
white anemones, and gorse
for kissing time,
slate flag steps, paths
of cobbles, another stone
for this dry Sussex cairn
she keeps.

No weathering process here,
just the fast train to London,
in search of words and buildings
and the smell of the Thames.

Smiler on Men's Surgical

Sister Boniface

Sister Boniface doesn't like me.
When we were in the mortuary
I expressed feelings about the dead
seeming like large rubber dolls.
She eyed me up and down. I knew
without any doubt at all that
Sister Boniface doesn't like me.

I don't like Sister Boniface,
and the patients all say this place
won't seem the same without me.
When they are all rubber dolls,
they won't know how I feel.
They call me Smiler, and pinch me,
but Sister Boniface doesn't like me.

Doctor

The doctor is busy taking his sex clinic.
On Tuesday nights he goes to CND
meetings and at weekends talks to bees,
and anyone else for that matter.

He's your real doctor all right.
Went to Cambridge and Barts,
larked about in the dissecting room,
went to medics' rags, laid a few tarts,
and anyone else for that matter.

He's an old man now, and last year
lost his prostate but not his marbles,
or his lusting stare – just his hair.
He fancies his own daughter-in-law,
and anyone else for that matter.

Good luck to him, I say. I don't
know what you say. I say Spain
changed him. Sometimes he's a pain,
but so is everyone else for that matter.

Porter

The porter's called Kevin and takes bets.
He's cheeky and Irish and young.
I follow the trolley and I know
he goes much too fast. The bookies
will be waiting for him,
and I would wait for him too,
if he should ask. I cry
a bit in the sluice, but he
just says, *Never say die*,
and takes my 50p.

Consultant

He has a hyphen between his names
and a knife between his shoulder-blades.
This is a fantasy knife and just a game,
but it looks very real. His shades
make him look so wise.

C.V.

Like an egg in huisenblas
he spent his first five months
multiplying his cells, floating
on a thin red string, pulsing
uneasily on the way to therapy,
unwilling analysand, two patients
for the price of one.

Like a zoo primate on show
he spent the next two years
caged behind bars at night,
strapped in a coach-built
carriage by day, hooked
on rose-hip syrup and benamook,
insomniac addict.

Like an offender in a borstal
he waited eight years for exeats
with a mute patience, keeping
his head down and his nose clean,
his crimes listed as school phobia,
timidity, cerebral bookishness,
symbiotic dependence.

Like an undecided transvestite
he did six years time, his hair long,
his gown black, his trousers flared,
encircled only by words, free at last
to find the final autonomy, abandoning
his thesis, living on the poverty line
in furnished rooms.

Mrs Perkins and Oedipus

Mrs Perkins lives in what she calls
a geriatric ghetto. She is a widow
who loves cats. The neighbours,
who are also widows, keep their houses
neat and clean. Her rooms smell
of cat pee and her pension she spends
on cat food and tins of soup
and books of poetry and vet's bills.

Her two tabby cats are called
Myshkin (Dostoevsky) and Masha
(Chekhov) but answer to Moosh
and Minka. Into this world
of scattered manuscripts and her dead
husband's journals and rejected novels
came Oedipus, a joke kitten
whose mother mated with her son.

Mrs Perkins sits in the vet's waiting-room
among the dogs and cats and their owners,
and a very small hamster on a wheel.
She is ashamed of having Oedipus "done",
as they say, or neutered as she says
to herself, to excuse this barbarous act.
The young vet looks round the door
and says 'Mrs Perkins and Oedipus'.

A cat's-paw of titters goes round the room
like a ripple on a calm sea, before a storm.

Girl with an Ermine

I like that one, he said;
girl with a mink it's called.
You must be out of your head,
she said, unless she had
a sugar daddy in da Vinci's time.
Sorry, he said, I made
a mistake; girl with an ermine,
not a posh fur coat,
but some kind of a stoat.

Casting Off

Where the day blurs at the edges,
I force my way through the hedges
of anger and the mutilating ridges
of ploughed fields, making my bridges.

A young nurse is crying in the sluice;
she will soon come to silently dowse
the lights in the Recovery Room, bruise
her eyes with make-up, shake her hair loose.

The student is phoning home; the course
is too hard, panic ruffles his voice
like cats' paws over water, his poise
is fragile as china. Wales was his choice,

but Swansea is as far away as trauma,
alien as the Socialist sixth-former
who watched the sun come up and warmed her
hands between his bony chest and pullover.

Where the sun goes down early behind
Maids Causeway I go away half blind
with grief, search in pockets to find
a tissue. They are two of a kind,

and demonstrate the need for her to cry,
and him to stay, casting them off by
stages, the bloodied knitting that I try
to forget as I comfort them with lies.

Workshop

The tutor has laid
the prettiest girl student,
who is in tears
and not writing a line
of poetry.

The young man who paid
his fees promptly
wonders how
he'll manage now
and is not quite sure.

He is not quite sure the staid
poetry he learnt at school
is what is in,
these days, or what is out
for that matter.

Two middle-aged women made
this trip, nurturing
ideas about the young Keats
and are in two minds
whether to stay.

The other tutor has frayed
trousers, and a lot
of hair, leaves out
punctuation
& likes ampersands.

In the evenings they played
a word game
to give the muse
a bit of a push.
It did that all right.

The last morning one stayed
behind to pick up
all the detritus
of wet handkerchiefs
and screwed-up poems.

Madam

The blinding white of the coral yard
is what she remembers, the fear
of black faces is what her mother
reminds her of, gently taunting,
skilled at flirting as if with lovers
who adored her, expatriate matriarch,
shifting beds around in her ninetieth year.

She is racist to the fingertips, says
she can smell a negro a mile off,
now feeds the horses in the fields below
this Sussex house, recites the names
of past West Indian governors, a litany
which her daughter adds to, shy, restrained
and not screaming wildly any more
as she did her first year there.

Colour and class are as important
as family and status, but words of love
are something they don't mention any more,
fondling the mushrooms she has picked
this morning, sharing them out carefully.
Madam, I take baby and stop her yell.
She is more her coloured Nanny's child
in spite of Roedean, Canada, Cambridge,
with her father's disposition to T.B.,
choking on bronchoscopy, than heir
to boss and lady, stumbling through fear.

At night she eats the entrails and the cut-out
hearts of slaves, like punishment,
like Madam's soft white mushrooms.

The Diseased Vine
A Poem for Four Voices

EMILY. I came here with Clarinda one autumn in a year
    Whose numerals have dissolved and fallen away,
    But whose season remains in my memory of fear,
    In the driven bead curtains of rain, in the sway
    Of a young girl's scarlet skirt, the skirt
    Of Clarinda treading the wet roads
    In a year which I cannot remember.

    I have always been happy. I have always found life
    Pleasant, loving hot coffee, and the conversation
    Of children, and long clean lengths of patterned
    Material tossed on mahogany counters, intoxication
    Of brilliant flowers gathered carelessly for a striped
    Jug, brick and tile and the sudden sight of a meal
    Laid in an empty room, traditional ancient knife
    And fork and spoon, plate and mug and wooden bowl
    Of ripe fruit. I could not understand that life
    Can sometimes like a garlanded albatross
    Hung upon the necks of the doomed.

QUENTIN. I remember that year. The leaves were stripped
    From the trees early, the gales came in from the coast
    Like an angry choir, the rain splashed and dripped
    On her hair as she walked with Clarinda.
    They carried a basket with a plaited handle,
    And gathered wood for the evening fires.
    She cannot remember the year now, but the handle
    Imprinted a plaited scroll on her bare brown
    Hand, I never saw the hand of Clarinda,
    Only, the long and slender arm and the frown
    Between her eyes, and the coiled blonde hair.
    I never looked at the palm of her hand.
    Yes, I remember that year,
    The year that Emily tries to hide
    From. The year the child died.

EMILY. That autumn my child lay poised and curled
    In his cage of bone. My thoughts circled
    And spun and swam around him, the pearled

Grasses broke under my heavy tread.
I thought of his weak mouth at my breast
When he moved like a dolphin as I lay awake
In the stone house with the vine. I thought of rest
After labour and the mid-wife crossing the lawn
With careful feet, calling Quentin.
I hardly saw the rue on the brow
Of Clarinda
But I think of it now.
I hardly saw the berries turning
Or smelt the damp leaves burning
On my walks with her.
We gathered wood in a deep basket,
I seem to remember,
And the handle bit into my hand.

CLARINDA. That year is a stone in the centre
Of my being, that terrible long year
Which bent me into a shape of fear
From which I shall never recover,
The year, we walked in the woods,
Emily and I, and the invisible child
Was our inseparable companion,
Becalmed in his locked waters
Like the ancient mariner in his pelvic cave
Hoods of grief over his eyes,
Hands crossed,
Turning,
Waiting.

At night the yellow cats crept into my bed,
Beau Soleil and her white-pawed kitten,
Blunt-headed against my naked breast and thighs.
Their pelts grew wet with my tears, their eyes
Observed me patiently.

In the mornings the coffee tasted bitter
As gall, voices pierced my skull,
Like a remote echo, asking if I
Would like to go for a walk, to hear
Some music, some more coffee. Fear
Was my invisible companion.
They seemed to be asking me if I
Would live or die.

Most days the rain speared the sodden lawns.
Quentin and I play chess, the pawns
Encircled the Queen on the lurid board,
A phalanx of fear played out
In a chilly room.

BENVENUTIO. That was surely the year Clarinda went into hiding
Spending a solitary vacation with Quentin and Emily
In that wretched stone house with the diseased vine.
I said I was afraid I should have to decline
Such a kind invitation – not a drink
In the house, only the wine
From the bitter grapes by the outhouse door,
And a mandolin hanging from the yellow wall
As you pass through the hall,

The ribbons clamp and lifting
In the draught.
I missed Clarinda, and thought of her
Suiting her restless pace
To Emily's pregnant roll.
I was glad not to see Emily in the family way
Perpetuating the race,
The noble human race,
The cream of the animal kingdom
With their Buchenwald
And Crackow.
I could see her face
Benign like a contented cow, and Quentin pruning
The roses to pass the time, and the yellow cats
Lying aslant the stone steps, and the evenings
Drawing in.

EMILY. It was cold that autumn. On wet days
Clarinda and Quentin played chess,
One day her tears streaked the chequered board,
And I thought perhaps it was her time on the month,
Or she couldn't afford to buy some new clothes
Or Benvenutio
Had left her.

Once, she played upon the mandolin,
But the ribbons were faded and rotten,

And the ghostly dissonance of a broken instrument
Floated through the open doorways.

QUENTIN. From the doorway the garden spread and grew,
   The roses bloomed in the moist damp air,
   Bud upon bud unfurled, their wet scent
   Pursued me. I thought of the sterile heat
   Of the Indian plains, and the savage grace,
   And the ravaged face of Clarinda walking
   Was the grace of a woman carrying a pitcher
   Of water in a foreign land.

BENVENUTIO. Water? Give me gin. When I am drunk
   Clarinda bends her proud coiled head
   And her proud cold hate melts
   In the fire of my drunkenness.
   Only then do I reach the core
   Of her solitary mindless wonder.

CLARINDA. I would have liked to walk alone
   Among the dead bracken, but Emily had
   To have a little exercise, she said,
   For her health's sake, she said,
   For the child, for the child.

One morning the sun shone in an unfamiliar
Sky, the hedges sparkled like the cheap
Ring Benvenutio gave to me, in Paris.
I put on my scarlet skirt and fetched the deep
Basket from the womb-like cellar
Where Quentin stored his wine.
My fear was like a cancer growing
To obscure me for ever. Quentin was hoeing
The vine, and the blotched leaves
Lay upon the damp earth like my love
For Benvenutio, and his face turned to mine
Was no longer Quentin,
Only a barbaric mask on a long pole.

After we had gathered the wood we sat upon a log,
Like a rustic scene in the musical comedies
Benvenutio goes to. Emily laughed and was happy,
And mended the broken strap

Of my sandal. I hear the snap
Of the thread as she broke it off.
I saw the trees like an advancing army.
I saw my hand raised in a salute.
I saw my hand push Emily out of
The darkening scene.

She jerked and fell and rolled a little way,
And hit a tree, and lay quietly with the curve
Of her belly turned towards the sky.
When I looked at my hand the mark
Of the basket handle was there still.

QUENTIN. That evening when the doctor had driven away,
    And the child was dead and Emily lay
    Under the embroidered quilt and Beau Soleil
    Played in the dusk with the white-pawed kitten,
    I tore down the vine from the outhouse wall
    And burnt it, the flames unwilling and the wood
    Too green.
    With the smell of the wood-smoke still on my hands
    I kissed her blind young face as we stood
    In the hall. I held her narrow wrist
    Between finger and thumb, the twist
    Of her hair made my eyes fill with tears,
    But I let her go without a word
    Back to Benvenutio.

    I shall never forget the swing of her skirt
    As she walked through the ash
    Of the half-burnt vine.

BENVENUTIO. She came back earlier than I thought.
    The rooms smelt of dust and beer

    And smoke. The sound of her sandals
    On the naked stair-boards filled me
    With a passion of love. No mistress
    Has ever been to me what Clarinda was.
    Her silences and her distress
    And her bitter weeping were part
    Of my love for her.
    When the rain
    Slides down the roofs and I start

To think of her, I remember her scarlet skirt
And the way she talked of the yellow cats
After that child of Emily's died,
And I feel the soft palms of her hands
Against my cheek
Again.

EMILY. Now, when the days draw in and the leaves rustle
  Over the grave of Beau Soleil, where the vine
  Once grew, it is hard to forgive Clarinda.
  I think of the wasted life of all but nine
  Months waiting, yet it seems the tragedy
  Was hers not mine.
  September is always a melancholy month for me.
  It rains, and Quentin prunes the roses,
  And somewhere I seem to hear a tune
  Played on a broken mandolin.

Vikings

They gathered at dusk, nerves stretched,
boasting and wrangling, their swords
sharp as a mother's tongue. Over the hill
they came shouting and yelling, raped,
pillaged, fired the quiet houses with torches,
watched the household gods melt and crack,
and one stumbled as he ran and fell,
blood on the flesh, spittle in the mouth.

When they came to the painted gates
the horns on their helmets made them
look six feet tall, until their mothers
hauled them in by the back door,
snapped their wooden swords, smacked
their tender bottoms, made them cry.
The fallen leader walled his way upstairs,
to antiseptic clouding the bath water,
while his mother washed his grubby jeans.

Outside, ashes settled on the lawn,
shadows lay in scorched shrubberies,
little girls lay shivering and curled
under patchwork duvets, dimmer switches
glowed all night, and the wounded one
picked at the plaster on his two-inch scratch,
sniffed the smell of roasting meat,
and was puzzled by his father's key
in the door, and the great shout of laughter
which echoed on the stairway like a war cry.

Communiqués from the Dog House

I was a faithful little hound, sat
when you told me, did my little business
in circumspect places, but O my master
I have forgotten the rules of the pack.

As I sit among my stinking pile of bones
I reflect that you always walked me
too fast, rapped out your curt orders,
bewildered me with double-bind commands.

I could have been a loving little bitch,
fawning on you, carrying your papers
in my soft mouth. Now that I lift my lip
can you be sure if I snarl or smile?

Master, I was never a noble animal,
just a mongrel with no pedigree or sense.
Nobody will enquire why you had me
put down, and I have no logical defence.

Come, loving sharpened needle, kindly vet;
I am ready to leave this dog house,
for you have extracted the sweet marrow
of a symbiotic life and I am eager to go.

Reports come to me of dog eating dog,
and copulating in the streets. I do not
know if this is true, shivering in here
on my short chain with my staring coat.

Too often on heat for your liking,
barking at the wrong time, and then,
to bite your hand! O my master
I disobeyed the rules of the pack.

Below the Snow-line

Up here the air is too thin,
a rarefied atmosphere, a fine
flurry of flakes below the snow-line.
Because of you they are all leaving
their husbands and lovers, and yet
it is strange; they are living
alone, or with their children,
and their poetry has changed,
like the weather in the Urals,
for now there's a threat of snow
and the clouds are heavy and swollen.
They all know there is only one woman
for you, although they pretend
that they will be remembered in poems
or novels or witty one-act plays.
Her pregnancies were when you
most needed them, but her births
draw him back to domestic days,
as she waits in her satin and lace,
slowly turning back the shawl
to show you your own face,
and hers and a hint of something else
as well. Your typewriter chatters
all night; she joins you quietly
for the night feed, flatters
you as the baby suckles, and goes
back to bed alone with no backward looks.
The new novel will soon be finished,
and all the shadowy women depart,
writing better, but sadly diminished,
planning their lives and their books.

Little by Little

Y knows that post-Franz X is sad,
despite her composure. It's bad
karma now but had been something else,
(like life, like some kind of glory),
but, as X says, that's another story.

Clichés like this suit them well
in the autumn evenings when they tell
each other that love and passion never died,
sifting their melancholy thoughts together,
walking after classes in misty weather.

The tutor is a slob they both agree,
and only in it for the money. He
doesn't hear those tender dropping notes,
cannot conceive that sob-stuff is OK
sometimes. He never heard F play.

Sometimes X and Y can't think who
is who, as if they both really knew
that love was an illusion and only lasts
for a season, like the Bach potions.
Eric aims to rid them of romantic notions.

He can't help his name, of course,
but tries to keep it dark. They force
it out of him, with Bernard's help
and cruelly use it whenever they can.
Y suddenly misses her quiet American.

The Mistress

The day of the funeral: in my dream
I was trying to kiss you through a fence
of meshed wire like a cat licking cream,
my tongue touching your surprised face.

The dance is done, the party's over,
the black skirt hangs over the chair.
I used to dress for meetings and my lover,
a frantic choosing and brushing of hair,

even when I was old and not worth
the time and trouble, for nothing hid
the lines and blotches or the girth
of an expanding waist-line. I can't kid

myself that you'll be looking down
at all of us shivering by the grave,
or that this pinched face, its frown
habitual, will seem serene and brave.

You know some of the answers at last
the minister says, but no cards to say
Wish you were here float slowly past
our line of vision on this chilly day.

Back at the tidy house we drink,
but not to your health. Sherry warms
us for a little while, but I shrink
from the touch of your wife's palm

on mine as I say my polite goodbye,
not believing that you're really dead,
but knowing how you went to earth
like any hunted fox in panting dread.

The Invisible Enemy

You never know when he will call,
flicking the lights off, treading
softly, smiling his vampire smile,
playing shadow games on the wall.

You will get up and offer him a cup
of tea, or if his meaning is too clear,
something a little stronger in a glass
and listen to his voice until sun is up.

He will pursue you until you cry
for mercy, and when you think at last
he has gone away, he will return
and help you plan the way to die.

He will show you the misty view
from John Keats before he goes.
This time he's had no luck at all,
but he will always remember you.

Counsellor

And why do you think you feel this way?

She listens, remembers the course tutor
and his list of rules, listens again, avid
for the exposure of weaknesses, the play
unfolding, the dénouement in Act Three.
She knows about role playing, body language,
the gently inserted questions, the flares
of anger, sorrow or contempt, and she
is privy to the shadow-play of fears
and guilt, the sexual longings and the pain.
She cultivates an air of calm and dignity,
keeps a box of tissues handy for the tears.

Sometimes at night she wakes suddenly,
lost as any traveller in an arctic waste,
reaches for the bottle by the bed; her chaste
body in the pristine sheets shakes.

In the morning she washes and dresses carefully,
eager for the faltering admissions skilfully
extracted – hints of sadness, signs of strain.
Hot on the scent she licks her lips a lot
with a clean pink tongue, uses the jargon well.
'Supportive', 'personal relationships', 'bereavements',
she tries out, using eye-contact and notes
the timing of the session to the dot.

Caught off guard even in the daytime, in her room,
her face dissolves into lines of anguish and despair,
until the next client opens the door and sits down,
displaying a black eye's multi-coloured bloom.
Her eyes shine (with sympathy, love and empathy).

How did this happen? Take your time. Tell me.

Songs My Mother Taught Me

You'll laugh on the other side of your face
meant tears before the day was finished.

Who got out of bed the wrong side
was the downward spiral, manic-depressive.

She thinks the world shines out of his arse
warned against love and devotion gone mad.

A pig with one car was her waspish comment
on a new-style tried out to impress.

Where was Moses when the light went out?
Down in the cellar with his shirt hanging out.

A lesson on sex, and who do you think you are,
The Queen of Sheba? was a quick slap-down.

And yet, as she fell on her knees to scrub
the scullery she sang, 'Thank Heaven for little girls',

was devoted to Maurice Chevalier, and made me
long to live in France, twenty odd miles away.

The Comforters

I'm sorry your wife is dead. Was it sudden?
No, I understand you wouldn't want to talk of it.
She was really quite young, I believe, leaving
children behind her, which, though I see you're grieving
is quite a responsibility. Yes, quite a responsibility.

You can see that while they live she is not dead.
It's something about the eyes, the set of the head,
a way the youngest has of going off screaming
to the bottom of the garden. Yes, I do see that;
not that she actually screamed. She just went away.

Please forgive me. That last remark was unfortunate.
Sometimes it appears as if the dead leave on purpose,
not there to do the washing-up, or pack trunks
for school, all those undone chores they leave behind.
They don't deliberately plant forgotten things for us to find.

As you say, that's not really the point at all.
It's too soon, yet, I do agree, to be objective.
No, don't look at me like that. Time will heal.
I only meant that time will... Yes, I know, I see,
but please don't throw the wrong ball back at me.

Night Songs from Waterloo

Pushing seventy, Birdie sings.
Trying out her new-found riffs,
upraised arms look like wings.
She ought to be among the stiffs,
her bad teeth, her stringy hair,
her wild look, her piercing stare.

Birdie doesn't know she's past it,
gets the audience on its feet.
Brash and tipsy, damn and blast it,
all her friends are now dead meat.
Her young voice belies her age
when she stands on her makeshift stage.

We love you Birdie, love you truly,
with your long black skirts,
your grey hair matted and unruly,
your patina of marbled dirt.
Sing us all to heaven and back,
before we fall into the sack.

Holding Up the World

It's no laughing matter, I tell you,
holding up this arch like Atlas
bent beneath the weight of the world.
Sometimes I groan and bray, a jackass
impatient under the load of the Nazarene.
Sometimes my forehead is pearled
with sweat, a hint of vinegar on my chin.
At Easter they will all come to view
my painted agony: one writes in the book
A lovely muriel. It's no laughing matter,
holding up the centuries, and if you look
a little closer, I'm cracking up fast.
How much longer can I last?

Photography Class

The dark room; hands-on experience;
black and white studies of a foot,
a gateway, a motor-bike.
Chris and Katarina are in their element,
making arty studies of life.
You can do what you like,
the tutor tells them, but
do it well.

The whole gang's here.
Mrs A brings her transparencies
(work that one out),
and Hugo with his nudes.
Dr Moon brings equine fantasies
and Cynthia and B
some impressionistic shots
of the Seine. Long John's
pensive photographs of kids
are not as innocent as they seem.
Zoe's into wild flowers,
but Alice captures endless shores
or equally endless skies,
laughs at Mrs Herriot's
poncey wedding groups.

The tutor? he aims
his zoom lens
at landscapes, claims
affinity with rocks and stones,
never pins down humans
in their natural habitat.
His topography is erotic,
but his wife is fat.

The Death Diary

Impossible to think of him silenced.
Impossible, for a short time, to imagine going on
without him, going alone to all the meeting places.

The barman makes his desultory small talk,
the lunatic bottles hang upside down,
saved from their suicidal tendencies
by his indifferent, but charitable hands.

Impossible to think that he would have enjoyed
the carefully prepared food after the burial,
or admired the privileged flowers living
disabled lives in their wire calipers
baring their heads in wedding hats
without any sense of occasion.

March is now the well-thumbed month
in the death diary. Impossible to think
it will ever be the brave precursor
of the Spring, releasing prisoners from the earth
like timid dissidents before the mass exodus.

He belongs with his letters in the desk drawer,
and with his poems in yellowing books.
Impossible to think I cannot call him hack
with satirical phrases and all that is left
of love and whisky and cocked-up obituaries.

The Burden

You carried burdens for a few years,
used them to demonstrate compassion,
retreated from them, laid them down
when the going got hard, evaded passion
of any kind, found that acting the clown
went down well, went back to easy pickings.

Sometimes you really went to town
on snowdrops and God, after the funeral
of the four year old, wept when your dog
did not exactly die, but was put down,
never knew the nine month's burden, or
the piercing cry, the row of mutinous kids
abandoned for the second time around.

'My dear,' you write, slapping me down
so gently and so quietly only I can see
the complacency behind the frown
of worry for me, which you wear so well.

Watching me sort out the laundry, you check
your linen carefully, matching shirts
of blue to blue, and brown to brown.
Of all the stains of blood and semen,
milk and tears, you own the last.

Moving on, I still find old love letters,
small limp toys, darned into life,
old forties magazines with thin and shattered
spines, the school reports, the marriage lines.

Do you still keep your mortar-board and gown?

Making Elegiac Noises

There's enough of blue
in the sky to make a sailor
a pair of trousers.
Well, you can't blame me
for thinking of this, with you
nailed down in a box
and the fierce sun
shining for an hour or two,
lighting up stone angels,
drab mourners like blackbirds,
the wounded earth
turned back, green flesh
pinned open for the surgeon.

There's enough of late snow
to seem like snowdrops in a blur
of tears, and a cold wind
to sting the eyes for those who
cannot cry. We are
sufficiently serious to mourn
your passing, but we know
that even your courage
faltered at the end.
As you jerk into the raw hole
we put on our funeral masks
inhaling the potent anaesthetic
of words, the lexicography of loss.